You Can Grow Rich

Think Your Way to Wealth

Edward Bartell

Introduction

Think and Grow Rich is one of the most influential books of all time in pointing the way to personal achievement - to financial independence and to riches of the spirit beyond measurement in money. Thousands of people have applied the famous philosophy of this book title for their own enrichment. Its secrets are as timeless and practical as when the first edition was published.

Table of Contents

1. Can You Really Think and Grow Rich

2. Think and Grow Rich - Crazy Concept or Great Advice

3. Do You Believe You will Get Rich in MLM?

4. Easy Ways to Grow Rich

5. What is Wealth?

6. What does Rich Mean?

Chapter 1

Can You Really Think and Grow Rich?

There are many ways to interpret Think and Grow Rich. This is just one way I see it.

Having read the book "Think and Grow Rich by Napoleon Hill" a couple of times I can highly recommend it to everyone. Whether you are looking to get rich or not, there are deeper lessons to be learned from it than how to grow rich by thinking about it.

I don't want to go into details of the book at this time, but just want to look at the title "Think and Grow Rich". Can you really Think and Grow Rich?. Well if you take a look at you own life to this point in time and work your way backwards step by step, you'll see a very clear pattern emerging.

Lets look at your present job for example, (fill in the blanks to suit - this will work for just about any job or position - employed, unemployed or other!) So, at the moment your a ___, and you've been there since ___. Before then you where a ___. Then you either wanted to change or had to change due to either your circumstances or those beyond your control.

Now this is the interesting part.... you got to your position today as a direct result of your thoughts! - If we take that a little deeper you'll see how that works and, how you can control your next move.

Lets make up some circumstances for a good example:

Alan works in a supermarket, and he hates it!, so he's faced with a decision that will change his life forever. This decision will be made either in hast or after some thought. Now if Alan just sits and thinks for a while he will begin to see the options he has, and the things he can or can't do. So Lets look at two scenarios:

Do nothing and put up with it. Requires no thought, and no change and is by far the easiest option.

Put some thought into his options and think more long term.

This could lead to all kinds of outcomes lets take a look at some of the possibilities:

   a. Look for new positions within the company
   b. Look for promotion within the company
   c. Look for a similar position with another company as he can do the job well, but just wants a change of scenery.
   d. Learn a new skill, one that he finds interesting and would open new door's for possible future employment, or even self employment.

This simple example shows just how useful a little bit of thought can be. Now this may seem obvious to some people, and may even appear to be stating the obvious, but until you break down the process of how your thoughts shape your future, you don't often realise just how powerful they can be, so looking at the title of Napoleon Hills classic "Think and Grow Rich" and the original question "Can you really think and grow rich? The answer is undoubtedly YES - but only if you choose to think the right thoughts that will put you in the path to enable you to grow rich. We become what we think about.

Is It OK To Think That You Can Make Money Online Today?

When you look for an online income opportunity, you will see many of them telling you that you can start making money on your first day or that you can literally get rich quick overnight. To tell you the truth, these statements are not so true at all. I mean, the only place where you can really turn rich overnight is if you play the lottery and win.

This is the only place where you can get rich overnight and become wealthy. I have seen many websites promote a lot of hype telling their visitors that they can make a few thousands of dollars in their first week online or even their first day.

I am here to tell you that it is not possible to even get close to making these kinds of amounts. This is a big lie. The biggest problem with these websites is that they let people believe that it can be a walk in the park and that it is so easy to make it.

A lot of people think that, for a very small investment (usually less then $100), they can get rich and make thousands in their first week online. The truth is that anyone can make thousands of dollars online but it does take work, time, energy, and financial investment in order to become a success story in the work at home and home based business industry.

Now, why is it so damn hard to to get rich quick online? First of all, like I mentioned before, it takes time, work, energy, persistence, and financial investment.

Even if you get your website up with a product that can bring you commissions, you still have to invest your time, money, and energy in order to get your site up and running. And because your website is like a store front, you need to bring in as many people as possible to it.

You cannot just build a website and hope that people will find it online. You need to invest both your time and money in order to bring visitors to it. I am not saying that you cannot get rich online, because you can. But it will probably take you a few years of building some sort of income that will keep growing and growing.

Two of the best options for you are affiliate programs and some sort of an online network marketing business. These 2 options can make you a lot of money over the years if you do things right.

One of the easiest ways to make it big online over a period of time is to find a great mentor who is already doing really well and do exactly what they did and are currently doing. You can usually find mentors like that anywhere online.

Some of them do charge a one time investment for their training so if you have an option to go with someone who has a good reputation, then do that. This will be the best way to go.

But again, you will not get rich overnight or anything like that. The 2nd critical thing that I want to tell you is that once you find a good mentor, do exactly what they say. Take action. Never give up. Stay persistent, and talk positive about everything that you do. If they are doing well, just know that it did take them time too.

They invested their energy, their money, and their time. They themselves did not get rich overnight and they are certainly not lucky because luck has nothing to do with their success.

Chapter 2

Think and Grow Rich - Crazy Concept Or Great Advice?

Today as I sat down at my computer I was wondering "what 10 things can a person do right now to grow rich in their life?" Here is a list of 10 things you can do right now to grow rich in your life:

1) Find out where your finances are right now: both assets and liabilities. Get your papers organized and your bookkeeping up to date. This will give you a snap shot of where you are at financially today.

2) Set up a monthly budget for expenses going out and income coming in. If possible, put away savings - even if it is a little bit. Remember, small amounts add up to big amounts over time, whether that be for savings (+) or for debt (-). Once you know your monthly expenses and your budget is balanced, put some of your savings into your investments.

3) Find ways to eliminate debt. Do you have immediate debt to pay off? If you do, make a plan to put a certain amount of dollars on your debt even if you can get a lower interest rate to pay off a big sum of money at a higher interest rate. Pay over and above the minimum payment to pay off your debt. Perhaps you can work at an extra part-time job or business purposely to get out of debt.

4) Go to work if you have a job and if you need a job, go find one. If you have a job, give yourself credit for getting up and going to work everyday. That is excellent. If you work on your own business,

continue to do that. If you have a job but still need extra income start a side business. There is always something a person can do, whether that be selling items at home parties, making an income through internet marketing or doing a service for someone. Keeping a good attitude is half the battle in persevering in what you are doing.

5) No matter if you are working or not, start a business on the side. If you are working right now, a side business will help you gain back some tax money because of the expenses you will incur from your business. If you are not working and need income, and you cannot get a job, you can still start your own business, even if it's temporary. Once your basic living expenses are met, start thinking of ways to increase your income so you can use it to invest in savings, stocks or bonds, mutual funds, and/or real estate.

6) Continue to increase your education. I believe we should always be learning marketable skills. If you are in business, what course can you take to increase your skills? What courses can you take to make yourself more competitive in the market? What marketable skills can you do to make money that people will pay you for?

7) Always work on health and fitness goals. "What does health and fitness have to do with growing rich?" you might ask. Good question. Health and fitness has everything to do with growing rich. Having good health and fitness gives people increased energy, a creative mind, and overall enjoyment in life. Studies have shown that good looking people make more money than people who do not take care of themselves.

8) Everyone should be attempting to market something. Find a niche that suits you and start learning how to market it. For some, selling

will come naturally; for most people, it is an acquired skill that you will have to learn. No matter where you are at, why it is important to be in the market place is because this whole world is based on buying and selling. "If you can't beat them, join them." No use always giving your money to someone else for something. Start acquiring money from others by selling something they want or need. Of course, keep it legitimate and above board.

9) Invest your money. Everyone has heard of investing their money, but a lot of people still do not grasp the importance of investing and therefore do not invest. Why is that? Investing your money simply means to allow your money to work for you over time and to allow your money to grow. All you need to do, is to go to a financial adviser that you trust, perhaps from your own bank, and learn what they have to offer. Go to 3 different financial advisers before you make a decision on how and what to invest in.

Many people say that they do not have any money left over, after they pay for everything they want, to invest with. That is the problem right there. They are looking for money left over to use to invest with. Instead, take a small portion of your money and invest first. Use the rest of your money for expenses and anything left over can be for "consumable goods" that you most probably do not need.

Of course, I am not talking about consumable items you or your family needs, but there is a lot of consumable items you do not need that are purchased out of habit. Instead, this money could go toward investments, even savings investments.

Always follow your intuition on investing. If you have a bad feeling in your intuition about an investment, do not do it. Most financial advisers will help a person with their comfort zone as to the amount of risk they feel comfortable in taking in their investments, measuring it to the age of the investor. If everything looks sound and wise and you feel comfortable about it, then invest. Believe it or not, our mind, feelings and intuition can lead us to what is a good investment or not. Follow that.

Also, never underestimate the value of saving a little bit of money here and there over time.

10) Do not expect to grow rich overnight or to win the lottery. The proverbs say that gathering a little at a time is a good way to grow rich. This concept of gathering a little money everyday and putting it into an investment that grows a little at a time, almost always grows money without fail. Sometimes people do not gather a little money at a time because they think it is too minuscule and will not amount to anything - so why bother.

The problem with that type of thinking is that not investing anything will add up to nothing over time and that is what you are trying to avoid. It is better to invest a little at a time than nothing at all. If you have a big windfall of money, then invest that as well.

Most of us want the big payday, what is known as "the big ship to come in". However, some people wait their whole lives for the big ship to come in and it never comes. Instead, it is better to gather money a little at a time and invest where and when you can.

Once you have enough money accumulated you can invest in real estate or stocks (retirement funds, mutual funds, etc). This may be the longer road to acquiring wealth, but you will feel secure and confident that your money is growing bigger over time in various places. Do not place your hope on the big elusive ship that may or many not come in. If it does come in, that is a bonus!

A Think And Grow Rich Refresh

Whilst some personal development philosophies come and go, the 'Think And Grow Rich' philosophy by Napoleon Hill has stood the test of time. Unlike other self-help approaches 'Think and Grow Rich' was based on a real study with hardcore evidence behind it. It offered firm concrete steps that could be easily taken by anybody who put their mind to them which remarkably work as well today as they did when they were first uncovered.

It is for the above reasons that you should make use of the summary of the steps laid out in 'Think And Grow Rich' and ask yourself if you are applying them to your goals. You see these steps are not just about creating money, they can be used to achieve any goal you desire. Remember thousands of people worldwide have proven them to work!

Step 1: Desire - Probably the most crucial step, this system won't work unless you select a goal that you have a real desire for your goal.

Step 2: Faith - Believe and know that you can achieve your goals and that you will hold them in mind no matter what.

Step 3: Make sure you write out your goal in present tense as though you have already achieved them.

Step 4: Be prepared to ask experts in the field for help when required and try and attain specialist knowledge.

Step 5: Play a movie clip in your mind of exactly how your life will be after you have achieved your goals. Play this movie in your mind everyday.

Step 6: Organized planning, make sure you have a well thought through written plan that you can keep referring to and form a mastermind group of people that can help you brainstorm and achieve your goal.

Step 7: Be firm and decisive, don't dither be clear on what you want, take action towards it and don't look back.

Step 8: Sure you can alter and modify your plan but never ever give up on your goals!

Step 9: Draw on the ideas and recommendations of your mastermind group. There is considerable power in the combined power of experts in a particular field or indeed anyone with similar goals.

Step 10: Work on modifying your beliefs so that they can support you in creating future success.

Step 11: Remember that your brain is similar to a radio station so use your intuition and listen to the universe so that it can guide you to the fulfilment of your goals.

Step 12: Acknowledge a higher power and be prepared to connect with it and tap into the infinite power that is available to you.

Chapter 3

Do You Believe You Will Get Rich In MLM?

Most people go through life wanting to get rich. This is why MLM is popular even with the image issues that exist. They want to have income coming in that they don't have to work for. They want to get to enjoy their lives and sit on the beach sipping their favorite beverage. If everyone wants these things why is it that less than ten percent of the population has these things? What makes that ten percent different from the other ninety?

It isn't education; there are millionaires that never graduated high school and they didn't inherit it either. It isn't social status; there are millionaires that started life in economically challenged areas.

So what made them different and set them on the path to achieve the goal that so many fail to achieve? You have a person in a MLM who can't make a buck. They sign up a guru that hits the top of the compensation plan in record time and has never been in a MLM before. If it isn't knowledge and it isn't status then what is it?

These aren't original questions - they are as old as man. While I am not intentionally copying another person's answers I am sure my own are not original. Go back in history as far as you can and you find have's and have not's and opinions on why. How can MLM help to change the have not's into have's? What sets the two camps apart and how do you switch camps?

The answer is their views, beliefs and filters - change your mind and you can change your world. The MLM guru has no doubt that he will succeed. They know they can do this either because they have done it before or because someone has drawn them a map of how to get from point A to point B that they know is accurate (whether it is or not doesn't even matter - it is the belief).

If you can succeed at doing something one time - just once - you can learn to do it repeatedly at will. It doesn't matter if it is hard. It doesn't matter if it is impossible. If you believe you can do it - you can.

It is impossible for a person with a shattered spine to walk again but some have. It's impossible for an athlete with a broken leg to continue to walk on it but some have. Why? They believed they could so they did.

I am sure that there are many of you both in and out of MLM programs who will disagree. You think it has to do with your why, the passion that you have, the training, your MLM mentor, the actions that you take or knowing what actions to take.

All of these things are important. None of these will happen if you don't have the belief. If you simply believe you can't build a massive MLM downline you won't. You simply won't take the action if you don't believe you can. They tell you in MLM you only fail when you quit and they are right. They are right because all it takes is getting it absolutely correct once and you can learn to do it at will. Why? What has changed in the world? Your belief in what is possible.

You have done it so now the belief that it is possible is an absolute. That will never happen if you quit doing MLM or anything else. It can't.

So where do you start? There are many books on these subjects available. Look for ones that reference changing your beliefs or neuro-linguistic programming. There are whole MLM message boards that talk about books that have helped people. Pick one that you believe will work. Then read it.

Studies show less than ten percent of the population, on average, reads past the first chapter of a book. Less than ten percent is rich. Is this a coincidence? I don't believe it is. Read the whole book. Do what it says.

Belief without action is a daydream. Believe you can change your mind. Believe you can change your world. Believe you can grow a massive MLM downline. Believe you can be a guru. Stop settling for what others believe is possible for you and you will do the impossible.

Chapter 4

Easy Ways to Grow Rich

Do you want to grow rich? There is NOBODY in this world who does not want to grow rich and you are not an exception. You are absolutely right that everybody in this world want to become rich. But 90% of the people don't have an idea on ways to grow rich. So, let us show you some good examples on ways to earn money and to become rich.

Invest and Get Rich:

Even though, some people might think that this method is only effective for people who already have some money to invest. But, they all are wrong. We are not talking about investing money here. We are talking about investing the time at the right place and on the right activity which can earn you money in order to grow rich.

Probably, this is the best activity in the world that can earn you good money and you will enjoy your success once you will realize the value of the time as it is already said that "Time is Money" and you actually making the saying true.

Affiliate Revenue - Grow Rich With Peace

Hands up if you love the stress and rush of everyday life? I bet not too many hands will be raised. Have you ever yearned to grow rich with peace? Working on your terms, when and where it suits you, employing incredible leverage, the kind that makes you rich.

In your dreams I can hear you say, but that is exactly it. You have to dream it and want it and then act on your instinct and believe that you will receive what you desire. That's how it works. That's what you have to do. If you want to grow rich with peace, claim it!

Once you've given your mind clear instructions, it will automatically go to work at making your wishes come true. Your brain cannot distinguish between reality and fiction so whatever you instruct it; it will move forward makine it come true. Suddenly you will find that you are open to opportunities, as your brain goes to work on making you grow rich.

The key here is to believe in the out come and then to do what it takes. It is here in the menial day to day action bits where we often lose the plot again and give-up. Realize you never know how close you are to that magical break through and if you quit you never will.

I absolutely love the saying that it is often darkest just before sunrise. Make you think doesn't. Nothing great has ever been achieved without persistence.

Did you know that stress is your enemy? It is bad for your health, it is bad for your mental well being and it positively clogs up your creativity, your ability to think freely, and will prevent you from achieving your dreams. Stress also drains the energy out of life, causes you to mismanage the relationships most beneficial to you, that of your friends and loved one's.

If you are sincerely interested in growing rich, you need to learn how to relax into a situation. Learn how to persist and follow your dreams even when instant results are not evident. And most of all, you need to persist with your plan until you achieve your dream or else you will never be fulfilled.

It will be amazing to see the results when you learn to relax and have fun in any situation. Undertake today to seek the fun part of life, dream, plan and persist and you will unlock achievement and riches in abundance.

Chapter 5

What is Wealth?

Everyone has their own interpretation of what wealth is and what it represents. This article touches on the topic based on things which I've learned and come to understand about wealth over the years. As a result, I've come up with the following conclusion.

Our lives are basically made up of four main attributes;

- Financial
- Emotional
- Physical
- Spiritual

The key to a successful and happy life is to try and achieve an abundance of all 4 characteristics. And in order to do so, the key word to focus on is "abundance" - to have more than is required for survival. In order to obtain an abundance of anything, you need to create a routine or system for generating that source attribute without the need of effort or the use of your time.

Below is an example of such systems or routines:

- For financial abundance you need continuous income
- For emotional abunadance you need family, friends and/or loved ones
- For physical abundance you need a routine or activities that you enjoy

- For spiritual abundance you need to have some sort of beliefs or rules that govern your life Financial Freedom

I'd like to take a moment to focus on the financial attribute as it is often the hardest to obtain. When you go to wealth seminars, read books and talk to people who have reached a substantial level of success, they will all tell you that the key to financial freedom is "passive income" - which is the ability to make money without exchanging it for time. In other words; to make money while you sleep!

If you can generate revenue without physically exchanging your time for money, you have successfully achieved a steady stream of what is called passive income. Now, that stream of income may not be enough to make you quit your job or become "fully independent" but what it does do is maximize the amount of money you're making while exchanging it for time. If you have something on the side that is making you money while your at work, you're on the right track.

It's funny... a lot of people just don't understand or comprehend the idea of making a living outside of the typical 9-5 work week. It never occurs to them to think of that as an option. They are too concerned with a safe, stable, reliable job and not concerned enough about a life full of freedom, choice and flexibility. They live to work, not work to live. This is why most people do not achieve true wealth and happiness.

Wealth does not mean money.. or being "rich". Although having an excess or "abundance" of money is a part of wealth, it's not the whole shebang. "Wealth" is the entire package... the "Qwan"... as Cuba Gooding Jr put in the 90's movie Jerry Maguire. You can a be a farmer or fisherman living in the Caribbean with a family and be 100%, absolutely, undeniably wealthy... more wealthy than Bill Gates. Why? Because you have shelter, an abundance of food, no "real" need for money and you have people to love that will love you back. It's a balance. But everyone has their own criteria for what they define as being the minimum necessities of life.

The higher your standards become, the more difficult it will be to obtain an even higher lever of abundance. But remember, anything is obtainable, you just have to want it that much more. Once you reach that plateau and you can finally say "I'm wealthy", the only thing left to be concerned with is maintaining that level of wealth.

Just remember that knowledge is power. Knowing where you are today and where you want to be tomorrow will get you there... its just a matter of time!

Chapter 6

What Does Rich Mean?

Sufficiency means having food, shelter and clothing. Being rich can be defined as having considerably more than enough, both now and indefinitely into the future, without dependency on work or chance.

But humans generally need more than the material basics of food in their belly, a roof overhead, and a shirt on their back. They need to give and receive love, companionship, and a degree of fulfillment/purpose. Being rich is all these things. But can we all be rich?

Attracting Abundance and Resource Scarcity

The study of economics is based on the premise that resources are limited and scarce. If that's so, it shouldn't be possible for everyone to be rich. But the teachings of abundance suggest everyone can have all they desire, simply by adopting the right mode of thinking.

In actuality the universe is infinite, but at any one time the resources available to humans are limited. However, the human potential is powerful enough to create vastly more value from these finite resources than exists at that moment. So how come we're not all rich?

Resource Distribution and Abundance

From birth we are each dealt a certain hand. The circumstances we are born into determine the resources we start with, and these vary widely from society to society, and within a single society. As well as the financial background of our family, we are each endowed with a particular set of talents and characteristics. A crude analogy would be that our family's wealth level determines our place on the starting grid and our innate talents the speed of our car.

But two further factors determine how rich we'll get. First is how well we play the hand we've been dealt, and our efforts and their effectiveness. Second is what's generally termed "luck", the range of external circumstances over which we have no control.

It may appear there is little fairness in the allocation of resources as many of the determinants are beyond our control. However the degree and direction of our effort does play a major role in determining our material success. Furthermore, from a Spiritual perspective our birth situation, talents, and the circumstances we encounter are not random but are pre-determined (partly by ourselves!) in order to provide necessary experience.

Conclusion

One secret to wealth is to have the desire "To Grow Rich". One must have the desire first before any other effects will come into being. There are many moving part that are needed to think and grow rich, and one of the first pieces of the puzzle is the desire. Desire is wanting, craving, yearning, aspiration, wishing for, and longing. Understand that desire is the force that causes people to take action. Without action, nothing happens. Therefore, you must decide what you desire. Once you have determined what your desire is, you can then proceed to think and grow rich. If you do not have a desire then you do not have a reason to do something.

www.ingramcontent.com/pod-product-compliance
Lightning Source LLC
Chambersburg PA
CBHW080821220526
45466CB00011BB/3643